We had this brilliant idea. What if you put 30 students into a classroom for one day and taught them how to craft good poems—haiku, free verse, sonnets, etc.—and just let them write about anything they wanted.

Allowed them to express their thoughts, feelings, ideas about their world. And what if, you equipped those students with the tools to actually publish a collection of those poems—in one day! Could they summon the focus and courage to accomplish such a lofty goal? Could we teach them how to do the write thing? Could we provide a literary experience that was fun, inspirational, and transformative? Could these students produce a...

bookinaday

Hatching Hope

Poems Written in Gold by the Elementary Students of Pauline Johnson Public School

Written and Published by the Students of
Pauline Johnson Public School
Mary Alice St. James, *Principal*
Pauline Johnson Public School
4350 Longmoor Drive
Burlington, ON L7L 2M5

in association with Book-in-a-Day
Kwame Alexander, Founding Director
Tinesha Davis, Senior Coach
Deanna Nikaido, Design Consultant
PO Box 21, Alexandria, VA 22313
www.bookinaday.org

bookinaday

ISBN: 978-1-888018-38-7

10 9 8 7 6 5 4 3 2 1

Printed in the United States of America

To the teachers of Pauline Johnson Public Elementary School, especially Mr. Colderley, for making this happen. We thank you so much!

Contents

Acknowledgements

We did this entire book in one day. We would like to thank all the Book-in-a-Day coaches: Kwame Alexander, Tinesha Davis, and Deanna Nikadio for making this possible. We could never do it without you. Also we would like to thank the staff at Pauline Johnson Public School and the Parent Council for their encouragement and support throughout this project.

Sincerely,

Pauline Johnson Public School: Grade four, five, and six students.

Foreword

My mother and father read to me daily. It made a huge difference in my life. The hopeful journeys, the hatching of ideas, and adventures, and mysteries, and phrases, and chants, and songs brought my then shy personality to life. Reading and then writing gave me a voice. The emotions touched and the road travelled have been experienced by our students at Pauline Johnson Public School. Deanna, Tinesha and Kwame have instilled in our student writers, the hope that they too can bring to life silence, hope, joy, pain and adventures that can only take reality by putting thoughts to text. Hope springs eternal through the stories of our children—keep writing so that your voice can be heard and your stories shared.

Mary Alice St. James
Principal
Pauline Johnson Public School

February 18, 2011

A Note From Our Teacher

I first fell in love with poetry when my grade seven teacher introduced me to the "The Road Not Taken" by Robert Frost. Almost half a life time later, my assignment out of teacher's college was to teach poetry to middle school children. My advisor reminded me as I left that day, "Poetry is good for the soul." Writing with these children as well as Kwame, Tinesha, and Deanna has reinforced that lesson. Every time I share a poem with my students or read one of theirs, I am reminded of my advisor's words. My soul opens up and I know writing is also the way to a better world!

Speak Clearly

when
you
stutter
splutter
sputter
stammer
stumble

get
a

pen
write
it
down

Chris Colderley

"Hope is the thing with feathers, that perches in the soul."
Emily Dickinson

Hatching Hope

When your room gets stuffy
And you open your window
Hoping for a cool breeze
And a nice scent
When you go down the stairs
Smelling warm, soft,
Freshly cooked pancakes
With a hint of maple syrup
Hoping they're for you
And not your sister
That's the feeling a baby bird
Has when it's hatching
Hoping to be successful
At what it's called
To do

Joshua G.

When I Was Five

I lived on a street
I could not live anywhere else
Because I was just a kid

I owned a Buzz Lightyear toy
And I owned a Spiderman shirt

I didn't get into trouble
Because
I always listened to mom and dad

When I turned 6
I still liked Spiderman
But I didn't like Buzz Lightyear

When I turned 7
I learned how to ride a bike
And I loved video games

When I turned 8
I still played with my bike
But I didn't like Spiderman

When I turned 9

I loved clothes
But I didn't ride my bike

Then I turned 10
The double digits
I forgot I ever liked Spiderman
I forgot I ever Liked Buzz Lightyear
I forgot that I ever had a Spiderman shirt
But most of all
I forgot that I listened to my parents

Daniel B.

10

WHEN I TURNED TEN, I felt a lot older than usual. I felt like I could now do all the things I had wanted to do when I was nine. I felt like I could stay at home by myself, go to the store by myself, and go bike riding all by myself.

I felt different, like I changed a lot. From a kid to a tween. I changed from Children's Place to West 49, action figures to skateboards and BMX bikes, and little kid games to playing any video game I wanted. I felt cool, like a gangsta!

But my little sister is a big problem because she can't play video games with me. She's five. And now that I'm older, I worry about how many times my sister will whine to me if she can't play the WII too. This is now how I feel as a ten-year-old.

Jimmy S.

I Remember My Grandpa Neale

I remember when
we took him in the yellow field
rolling his wheel chair around the sidewalk
him making a little smile
2 years after his stroke

telling him about
how I did at school
and how I did in sports.

And every night before
I went to sleep
I prayed for him not to die

Neale B.

A Penny's Travels

You were a penny in someone's pocket.
You were a skydiver without a
parachute.
You were a wheel rolling down the
street.
You were a person getting kicked
by a monster.
You were an airplane flying in
the sky.
You were a heli crashing
into a sewer.
You were a swimmer
in the ocean popping
up for breath.
You were a fish
washed up on an island.
You were a bowling pin
getting hit by a ball.
You were
someone's grave
underground
and the people there
singing for you.

You were a penny and
always will be.

Ranbir B.

Ode to Girls

so pretty
like gentle swaying flowers
so beautiful
like a sunset drifting over a beach
So amazing
like a new kite flying in the sky
girls, they light my day
every day

Jake M.

Red Envelope

My mother
gave me
a red envelope
on the night of
Chinese
New Year's Eve

I touched the envelope
smoother than wax paper
edges so dull
it wouldn't give you
a paper cut

I stared at it
I was
hypnotized
by its glossy starlight
red like the
healthiest
red rose

I peeked inside
saw an emerald green
lucky 20 dollar bill

I wondered what luck
this would give me
I tucked it under my pillow
for the night
closed my eyes
and relaxed on my bed

Wendy Lu

Rocky Raccoon

Rocky Raccoon, he lives in a city
And I got to say he looks mighty pretty
Big black bands around those eyes
It's really hard to say goodbye
But don't worry Rocky Raccoon
I'm sure I'll see you around here soon

Jack D.

Ode to My Hockey Stick

Patterned like
A checker board
The flex makes it like a
Elastic band
The black tape is so dark
It hides the black puck
From the goalie's
View
The letters
Greener than grass
The invisible
Grip tape clear as water but
Stickier than super glue

Mitchell G.

The First Time I Went Skiing

"BUT MOM what happens if I fall and all of the kids laugh at me?" I whined.

"Please stop whining Cooper," my mom pleaded. We had just walked out of the equipment rental booth and we were walking towards the bunny hills. I was nervous beyond belief and I kept asking to go to the bathroom. As we reached the bottom of the bunny hill, Mom said it was time to put on our skies.

"Mom how do you put a ski on?"

You stick your foot in like this Cooper." My mom placed her boot on the ski. CLICK, the ski snapped onto Mom's boot. I did the same thing and when I lifted my boot the ski came with it.

"Come on Cooper," my mom called. I stumbled onto the lift pad.

When I reached the top of the bunny hill I stumbled off the pad and fell on my face. My mom skied next to me and helped me up. I stumbled along to where my mom stood at the edge of the hill.

Before my mom could speak I accidently tipped down the hill. I must have beginners luck because I made it down most of the hill. I didn't know how to stop so I panicked and fell leaving my skies two feet behind me. I got up and walked up the hill to my skis and picked them up.

SWOOSH, my mom stopped next to me. "Cooper you're supposed to bend your skis inward," Mom laughed.

We tried the hill a few more times and each time I was more successful than the time before.

"Now let's go to the lodge and get you warmed up" Mom suggested.

"Mommy I have to go to the bathroom," I exclaimed as we walked to the lodge.

"Not again Cooper," my Mom whined.

"Yep." And, I ran inside, fear gone.

Cooper W.

I Remember

I remember
the first time
I went skating
so slippery,
so scary,
so exciting.
My tiny
three year old feet
on the ice.
Slipping and sliding
clenching my mom's hands.
Looking at people skate
made me feel
tempted
to skate too.
I let go of
my mom's hand's
and took
my first step
on ice.

Annie G.

Ode To My Hockey Skates

my hockey skates
gray
like an elephant's foot
blinding me as I turn
blade digs into the ice
taking off the top layer
skate marks
my feet move
feeling crunched
like a boulder on a bug
my skates are tight shoes
with blades I balance on
feeling like I'm going to fall
when I turn
speeding by everyone
my skates are one of the best
things I have

Brendan C.

When It Snows

some kids stay
outside
to play
parents like to stay
inside

It's the season for
hot chocolate
giving
hockey
family
the pleasant time
It's winter time

Zach K.

Ode To My Soccer Ball

My soccer ball blasts off
like a rocket
when I kick it
and it flies
through the air like a shooting star
a tornado
that gets faster and faster
it zooms
around the soccer pitch
like a cheetah
running at full speed
until it bumps into a tree
and stops

Dalton B.

Ode to My Apple

I got to school
opened my lunch pail
a juicy apple was waiting for me.
I picked it up,
the skin felt smooth.
I took a bite and
heard a crunch as I chewed.

Lydia B.

Ode To My New Blanket

My new blanket
is gentle
as a newborn puppy
dense
like a nice
veggie sub.
I huddle on it
like my favorite
stuffed animal
newly washed.
I wrap myself
around it.
It feels like flames,
bright red and orange
flowers
big as fantastic fireworks

Deniz D.

Ode To My Toboggan

My dad bought me
my first sleigh
we went to the hill
right away
I went as fast
as a rocket
held on
so tightly
I pulled the
brakes with my tiny little
three year old hands
and came
to a sudden stop
I ran up the hill
as fast as my little
legs could go
to the top.
I went again
my dad pushed
me and hopped on
to the back
we went so
fast we won
a race

my dad said it's
time for your last
ride for now
it went really fast
I felt the breeze
go right though me
I thought to my
self that
it was so fast
that even
speeding bullets
couldn't beat me.

Justine L.

The Slimy One

“I CAN’T BELIEVE I have been sitting here on the dock for hours and haven’t caught a thing,” I said. I flung my colorful small sunfish back into the clear but smelly river. I dragged it back and forth through the seaweed, hoping to catch a big one. I watched the pike slither through the water like a slimy snake and “BOOM!” The pike pounced on the bored and sleepy sunfish (pumpkinseed). The red and white bobber sank under the filthy water. “Errrrrrr,” I tried to pull it out as I stood on the broken dock using all my strength. I was shocked because my muscles weren’t strong enough to pull the heavy pike from the water. Water flicked up and hit me in the eye and blinded me, I thought I was going to fall in. The weight from the pike was bending my small grey kid sized fishing rod.

I turned my head and yelled towards the cottage, “Dad please come and help me land the big one!” My dad is stronger than me so he pulled the pike out of the river. I watched the slime drip from the twenty four inch pike that my dad held in his large muscular hands. I was shocked to see that when we used our scale from the tackle box the pike weighed four pounds.

We put it in the water as it appeared to be dying. My dad held it by its gills. I didn't want to hold it as it looked so slimy and heavy. We took tons of pictures of my great catch of the day. My dad threw the bloody, bitten almost dead sunfish back into the water. It floated away with the rivers current. I thought a Blue Heron would eat it.

I really wanted to stuff my big catch because last year I caught a three and a half pound bass. These wonderful catches all happened on the same dock. I really wanted to eat the pike for dinner but my dad said it would be a boney delight.

My dad gently placed the four pound pike back into the river. As the sun was setting I watched it sink to the bottom. My dad poked it to see if it was still alive and off it swam. I thought to myself, "How many pike are out there in the Severn River?"

Joel V.

Ode To Water

Soft luscious water streaming
from the faucet
like a wet rainbow
in your
mouth as if you were
in heaven
or swimming
in chocolate
but you are really
just in water.
As small
as a raindrop.
As big as a tsunami
so big and so wet.

Brendan D.

I Remember

I remember the beach
where I built my big sand castle.
The shiny blue salt water sea.
When I put on the cold sun screen.
When I kicked the black and white soccer ball
with my mom and dad.

Max L.

Ode to My Favorite Chair

I had to sit on it
It captured me like
a sticky plate of honey
pulling me like a spectacular
magnet when I opened the door
in that chair
I was as light as air.

Caleb K.

Ode To A Cat

My cat sat in a chair
like a king on his throne
as still as a stone statue
not even moving the tiniest muscle.
Staring at me like a hawk spying its prey
without even blinking when petted.
He purred softly like fizz coming out of a soda.
His fur felt like the down, soft like a fluffy towel.
Once the petting stopped, the room went quiet.
Not even the tiniest sound could be heard
Then he jumped off the chair
wandered away into the distance
until he could not be seen anymore.

Colin K.

Ode To My Polka-Dot Hoodie

My friend handed me
a shiny pink bag
for my birthday.
Inside was
a dazzling
polka-dot
hoodie.
I put it
on lovingly.
It felt like a
cat's velvet ears,
cozy like hot cocoa on a cold winter day,
and it was as eye catching as a bright orange sunset
on a summer evening.
Its best feature
the pink and purple
polka-dots!

Alexandra N.

Ode To My Green Blanket

my mom
walked
through the door
with a big
green blanket

when she gave it to me
and it felt like
I was at the zoo
stroking a sheep's
woolly back

the soft green fur
brushing against my hand
felt like
sitting near the fire
petting my dog's
soft fur

Shannon W.

Ode To My Shoes

My mom said to me
I think you need a
new pair of
shoes
my old ones
so small and
so ripped

My 5 year old feet
trying on those
nice princess Velcro
shoes
my mom doing them up
so tight just like a thread
going through a needle

I slipped my
right foot in
said I love
them
please please
can you buy them

I wore them to

school the next day
every one thought
they were really cool
I ran across the room
so excited

I was so disappointed
that they didn't
fit anymore
when I turned 7

Rachel W.

At the Start Line

THAT RUSH of adrenaline flew through me as I got into place at the start line. I watched the ten-year-old girls run towards the first turn as I imagined myself going through the same stress as they had in a couple of minutes. My archenemy, "The Long White Line," just sat there waiting for that gun to go off. All of a sudden the starter made an announcement. "I have seen enough of the other runners pass so we will start any minute now," he spoke into the microphone in a low monster like voice.

I was even more nervous than before. Why did he have to make that announcement! I thought in my head. I started to settle down as the starter took his position at the left side of everyone. This is where he usually stood.

"Okay everyone. I'll say feet together, then stand up straight, I will raise my arm, and the gun will go off," he explained thoroughly.

He stood facing us on an angle as he announced. "Feet together," I was getting ready to pounce, "Stand up straight," his arm raised with a ninety-degree bend at his elbow, and BANG! We were off. I heard hundreds of feet pound as I ran towards my destination, Island Finish Line. The first turn was ahead of me.

"I can make it," I thought to myself as I was so close to the turn now. I could see the most known part of the course where it turns to a mulch and leaf path, the forest.

"Hey! I pushed a guy and he tripped!" Someone said to a teammate in the distance. I felt sorry for him but I knew I had to move on.

It was a cold day but otherwise it was perfect weather. I huffed and puffed.

"In through the nose, out the mouth," I repeated to myself. Other runners were entering the forest and I figured I was in about fifteenth place, but I wouldn't know for sure until I finished. I pictured myself crossing the finish line as I got the first place ribbon but I knew I would have to push harder to get it. I pushed myself even harder as I started to slow down to an even pace that I could jog at.

I entered the forest as I heard the crunching of leaves under my feet. I saw red, yellow and orange leaves fall from the trees. Sunlight shone in my eyes as wind pressed against my cherry red face. I was chilled right down to the bone. In and out, in and out. Oxygen flowing through my lungs, my feet pounded. Thump, thump, thump.

"It's time to run a race," I said to myself and there it was, daylight.

Eric O.

The Race

I COULDN'T FEEL my legs. My heart was pounding out of my chest. But I knew I needed to carry on with the race. I started getting a cramp, but I could not stop. I could hear the PJ students cheering me on. I was stumbling on the wet grass, slipping on the curve, afraid that I might slip and lose my place, or come in last. I had to put my fears behind me, while I turned the curve, hearing the PJ students cheering me on.

While I was running on the bumpy grass, I heard my coach telling me, "Josh you're in eighth place." I was so excited, but I knew it was just the beginning of the race. I ran faster, and faster, until I couldn't feel my legs anymore. But it didn't stop me from running my fastest. I ran faster and faster, passing people one by one, until I got pushed to the ground.

Ten people passed me. I was so angry I picked myself up and ran like I never ran before, passing runners in front of me. I felt good when I past the person that pushed me. It started getting crowded; it felt like a herd of bulls. I couldn't stop. I ran and ran and ran - side to side - making sure I kept my spot and trying to beat the person in front of me for a better spot for my team.

I ran faster and faster I passed more and more runners. I went uphill and downhill running as fast as I could. Finally the finish line was in sight. I slowly jogged up the last hill. Someone passed me, so I ran as fast as I could with the wind blowing in my face. We were tied but I leapt over the finish line. I was so excited when I got my eighth place ticket. I gave it to my teacher and I walked to get my bag, and then walked to get my ribbon.

It was so nice to walk again. I walked to get my picture taken. I walked to the bus, then onto the bus. I thought of all the things that had happened in the race and pictured the look on my mom's face when she sees my ribbon. She will be proud.

Joshua G.

Ode to a Soccer Ball

so much power
and
force when kicked
like the speed of a
bullet ricocheting
a couple of times
off metal

the best ball
is the only ball I will use
to play like
a
pro
soccer player

Jason L.

A Penny

You were a clean penny in a pocket
you were put in a bank
you went through a lot of mechanics
when you got out you were traded for a bill
you were given to a younger kid
you were dropped in the drain
and went to the sewer
you were all rusty
when the sewer cleaner came
he saw something shining
in the water
he picked you up
and you were loved all over again

Jeremy M.

When I Met Devyn for the First Time

I try to remember
When I met Devyn
For the first time
But I can't
And all I have
Are pictures
Of when we were babies

Devyn had
Very little hair
Chubby cheeks
Bright blue eyes
Little hands and feet
And she was so tiny

Every now and then
I look at the pictures
And try to remember
When I met my best friend Devyn
For the first time.

Alexis C.

My Degus' Death

from happy to sad
the night went by
sorrow filled my eyes

I held in tears
I walked upstairs
sorrow filled my eyes

he was gone
my little buddy
went to that cage
up in the sky

I miss you little buddy
sorrow fills my eyes

good-bye buddy
sorrow fills my eyes

Erin D.

I Remember

my old house being built
skeletal bare with wires
mysterious as can be
as I stand at its steps
I wonder where my
room will be
skeletal almost no
walls but it
does not topple
at all even
though it is so
tall there
with no
walls

Alec G.

Leaving

I remember the airport
saying goodbye to all my family
I was holding in the tears so much
I didn't want to talk.
they wrote me little notes saying goodbye.
Gave me hugs and kisses that made me want to cry.
Walking up the steep ramp
feeling nervous inside.
My family said don't cry
I wanted to go back
I knew it was too late
we were on the plane.

Zoe R.

Foggy Newfoundland

Foggy Newfoundland on my
grandma's rocky drive.

Daddy said "Give me a hug!"

I tried to be a big girl and keep
the tears inside.

My daddy said to me
"Never let go I will always
be in your heart."

I felt sad. Because that was my
last hug from my dad.

He drove up the black rocky
Drive, waved and
said to me with a smile,
"I love you!"

Olivia T.

Canada's Wonderland

ON SATURDAY, OCTOBER 17, 2010, I went to Canada's Wonderland. Had to wait a long time to get in, but had the whole day to go on rides. My dad, my sister, and I rode almost everything. My favorite was the Behemoth. Then second was the Bat. I liked it when it went backwards. Awesome! My third favorite ride was Skyrider. I liked that we were standing up while going upside down. That was very cool. My fourth favorite was the Minebuster. It's a wooden rollercoaster and it went really fast, but not as fast as the Behemoth. Another favorite ride was the 3-D Spongebob. When he ran over stuff the chairs moved as if we ran over the things too. After we rode all the rides, we went home. Dad bought me a stuffed animal that looked like a girl Snoopy. He got it so that I wouldn't forget the day we went to Canada's Wonderland.

Kathleen G.

An Ode to My Bike

A two wheeled monster
fast like a thunder bolt
makes my legs tired
until I can't feel them anymore

I wait
until my legs feel better
then   ride
my bike again

I go downhill
feel the wind blowing back my
long black hair
and when I go up hill
I feel
like I am going
slower than a
sloth

I pull my handles
I push my handles
it helps a little bit
but my legs are still

sore from the last time

when I get home
I walk up to
my room and
fall down on my old
bed.

Jefferson L.

On Moving

Moving away
Out of the country
Vehicles taking us to an
Interesting new city
New friends
Good-bye
old house.

Jack D.

Pebble

You were a pebble
Dropped from the sky
Away in the wind
Going to die

You were a pebble
Drifting in a stream

You were a pebble
Stopped at the bank

You felt you were in the jungle
Alone

Then you drifted back into
The current

Finally you stopped in the grass
No more water
At last
And never going back

Emily L.

I Remember

I remember the last time I had ice cream
The last time I had gym
The last time I watched TV
And the last time I had chips

I remember the last time I rode my bike
The last time I saw a bunny
The last time I had candy
Even the last time I had a cat
I remember my first step
But my favorite memory's yet to come

Dylan S.

An Ode to My Toad

My toad is a stuffed animal
That I sleep with every night.
He has a big mushroom on his head
I love him so much.

Cole B.

Ode to My Boat

I took
my boat
to the pond
turned the motor on
it made a sound
loud like a
hungry spinning
tiger shark
it cut through
water blue
as the sky
it splashed
all over my face
I returned to shore
went back to my cabin
I was so sleepy
without changing into my
pajamas I slumped into
bed

Mobeen R.

Bobcaygeon

THIS YEAR'S VISIT to Bobcaygeon was my favorite. The air was just warm enough to go swimming in the lake. My Mom has friends up there who live about a quarter mile into the forest, right beside a lake in a larger than average house. You could look right out a window and see the lake twinkle in the sunrise. But when the lake is dark and still it seems to be a bottomless pit.

This year my mom's friends weren't home, so we had to walk around town. We stopped by an ice cream store and bought some ice cream. After we ate we went to James and Shauna's house. They are also friends of my mom. Getting there takes a surprisingly long time considering how small the town is. When we got there they weren't home so we waited. It only took ten minutes until Shauna and her children, Foster and Calder, got home.

"Can we go fishing?" Was the first thing my sister asked. I thought to myself that she was being very rude.

Shauna answered, “Sorry, but we don’t have any fish in our lake.” Then Shauna added, “Just kidding.” We all went out to the dock. I fished there with a lure for the first time. Everyone else used worms.

We had supper on the dock. Lasagna and garlic bread. It was a very good dinner. Then we went inside. We watched some TV and basically went to bed.

The next morning, we went to the dock and fished. I used a lure again and everyone else used a worm. Then Mom and Shauna went to the store. While they were gone my dad cast out and thought he snagged a tree, but he actually caught a large small mouth bass—probably one of the biggest fish in the lake!

Later, Foster, Calder, my sister and I went in a row board and went all the way across the lake into the marsh. We couldn’t go far into the marsh because the boat was too big. So when we got back, I went all the way back to the marsh in a kayak. For dinner, I brought back a lily as a center piece for dinner.

That night, we went out on the dock and looked at the stars. There had to be at least a trillion. After a while I saw one shoot. I made a wish. I like Bobcaygeon a lot!

Jack H.

I Remember

My Nanno
Was a brave man
He was 96 years old
When he died
On my birthday
The worst day
Of all.

Hailey S.

Ode to My Apple

I opened
my lunch pail
there sat a juicy
red apple
that shined so much
I could see my reflection
a circle that could roll to the end
of the earth

I took a bite
sweet juice
came out like a water fountain
that tasted like candy
I ate till I could not
eat any more
I walked
threw out the core
realized I'd never have
an apple as
good as
that one

Zoe D.

An Ode to My IPhone 4

Rectangular shaped
Longer battery life
Silver chrome around the sides
Has a Hurley case with mixed
Colors
Touch screen
Lots of apps.
Brand new
Fourth generation
Front and back camera & video camera
Lots of fun
Sixteen gigs of memory
Newest model
Really, really expensive
Lots of games to play
Each Tuesday
New apps.

Zackery B.

A Rock's Journey

You were a rust colored rock with
moss.
You were a rock in a
machine that crushes rocks.
You were a brick
going to be smothered with
concrete.
You are a house with people living
inside.

Robbie K.

Life

it's sometimes
stressful with all the
writing and numbers

wherever you look
something is going to
happen

even if
things look
normal

things aren't
always what they seem

Kelsey Z.

Ode to My Chihuahua

My little brown dog passed through the hallway
flopped on the couch like a human falling asleep
stared right at me, and then fell asleep.
I patted his soft, fluffy fur.
He hopped off the couch
licked my cheek
like a free river.
Waiting for me.

Jeremiah H.

Ode to a Dog

I opened the door
out jumped my dog
slobbering with joy
running, jumping,
and barking with glee.
Smelling like wet dog
and a pinch of mints.
We played.
Jumped all around played fetch,
then tag got tired but stayed on
our feet until we dropped.
We tried to get up for dinner
but fell asleep.

Courtney B.

Mackem's Accident on the Floor

THUMP! MACKEM flipped off the chair and fell down right on the floor.

"Mackem," Christine, my babysitter, said with anger in her voice. "Come here, NOW!" Mackem's hazel-blue eyes looked like he was scared and his nose turned pink as he quietly walked over to Christine. "What is this?" Christine pointed to Mackem's mess beside the brown cabinet.

Mackem looked up at Christine and ran the opposite way. I chased after him as fast as I could. The little puppy darted everywhere. It took about five minutes until I could grab his yellow collar and pull him over to Christine.

"Thank you Devyn."

Christine stood up looking at the mess that was still on the kitchen floor and then the orange, yellow, pink, and red dog treats on the counter. She slowly walked to the sink and grabbed some paper towel.

"Come Mackem, come," I said patting my knees.

"Oh my, he hasn't gone in the house since I first got him and that was when he was sick. He must have really needed to go," Christine said. She picked up the mess and washed it around with water. "Would you like to feel it?" Christine said sounding sarcastic.

"No thanks," I said back.

Christine went downstairs and grabbed Mackem's leash. "Its 9:30. When I come back in I want you in bed, Devyn."

"Fine," I said.

Christine opened the door and started walking out.

"Wait, can I feed Mackem one dog treat before I go to bed?" I asked her.

Christine looked back at me and nodded her head.

Devyn M.

An Ode to My Dog

My dog ran by me like a cheetah
chasing prey
ran to its cage
and licked its paws
like a lion after a kill

I grabbed the toy on top of her cage
threw it across the hall
she got it and came back to me
we had a giant tug of war battle

She pulled as hard
as love pulling
on someone's heart

Joshua P. M.

Ode to a Turtle

At the cottage
I saw a small painted turtle
just sitting and
bathing in the hot sun.
It looked very scared
was upside down
could not get away.

I picked it up so lightly
that it almost fell from my hand.
It was so soft
it felt like a blanket against my palm.

I thought its mommy left
it in the middle of a hot rock
on the beach shore.
As I held it in my soft hand,
it kept kicking and scratching.
I could tell it was mad.
I set it down so lightly
it did not make a mark in the hot sand.
It started to run furiously to the water
I worried that fish would eat it as soon

as it went into the cold lake.
It had just hatched and
was only the size of a quarter.

I picked up the painted turtle
it was calm and tired.

I put the turtle in a tank
to keep it safe
I still have the turtle
three years later.

Samantha B.

About The Students

Ranbir B. is in grade 4. He likes to play and learn on his computer.

Daniel B. is in grade 5. In his free time he likes to play hockey.

Neale B. is in grade 5. He likes to play video games.

Zac B. is in grade 5. He loves to skateboard and play on his IPhone 4.

Alexis C. is in grade 5. She likes to write poems and sing with friends.

Erin D. is a grade 5 student involved in cross country, choir and drama. Her interests include reading, writing and singing.

Deniz D. is in grade 4. She likes basketball, gym, fitness games, and art. Her favorite activities include going to the library, going to the park, and playing with her sisters in the backyard.

Jack D. is in grade 5. He likes to play with friends and Air Soft.

Brendan D. is in grade 5. He likes to game it up on his PS3.

Alec G. is in grade 5. He likes to read and play video games.

Annie G. is a 5 grade student involved in basketball, track and field, and cross country. Annie also enjoys singing, figure skating, and break dancing, as well as bike riding with my friends and taking short jogs at night.

Kathleen G. is in grade 5. She likes to play video games and have fun with her dog.

Josh G. is a grade 6 student involved in basketball, soccer and volleyball. His interests include watching Premier League Football and cheering for his beloved, Manchester United.

Jack H. is a grade 5 student. He likes to watch television, participate in school activities, and play basketball.

Zachary K. is a grade five student involved in sports and many school activities. His interests include hockey, baseball, basketball, and video games.

Caleb K. is a grade 4 student involved in clubs and activities throughout the school. He enjoys playing sports anytime. Caleb also likes to collect hockey cards and coins.

Jason L. is a grade 5 student involved in basketball, soccer, hockey, and video games. He likes watching and playing the game Minecraft.

Justine L. is in grade 5. She likes to skateboard.

Max L. is a grade 5 student. He is involved basketball, hockey, and soccer. He loves to play soccer at recess with his friends. When he's older he wants to be a soccer champion.

Wendy L. is in grade 4. She likes learning, art and team sports. Her interests include knitting and playing video games.

Devyn M. is in grade 5. She has a passion for figure skating.

Jacob M. is in grade 5. He enjoys playing football. He would like to get better in math.

Eric O. is in grade 5. He is a musician and likes to play hockey.

Zoe R. is in grade 5. She likes to play on the computer and sing.

Hailey S. is in grade 5. She loves horses and horseback riding.

Dylan S. is in grade 5. He likes to play sports.

Jimmy S. is in grade 5. He likes to travel on his heely shoes and skateboard.

Olivia T. is in grade 5. She likes to write and draw.

Joel V. is a grade 5 student involved in football, soccer, Cubs, swimming, basketball, ball hockey, cross country, volleyball, writing club, think bowl, and Silver Birch. His interests include writing, reading, riding his scooter and bike, participating in and watching sports, and cheering for the Miami dolphins and the Dutch national soccer team.

Rachel W. is a grade 5 student involved in sports such as soccer, volleyball, basketball, and swimming. Her interests include reading, skateboarding, and playing with her friends and family.

Cooper W. is in grade 5. He likes playing video games and reading.

Kelsey Z. is in grade 5. She likes to skateboard in her free time.

About Our School

Pauline Johnson Public School is located in Burlington, Ontario, Canada. It is a Kindergarten to Grade 6 facility educating almost 300 students in the Longmoor Community. The school was built in 1967 and named after the writer and entertainer, Pauline Johnson, the first Native American poet to have her work published in Canada.

About Book-in-a-Day

Book-in-a-Day (BID) is a groundbreaking poetry and publishing program aimed at elementary, middle, and high school students. Launched in 2006 by Poet & Publisher Kwame Alexander, the program teaches students how to write and publish a book of their own poetry—in one day. visit www.bookinaday.org for more information, or contact Kwame Alexander, Founding Director at kwame@bookinaday.org.

7725679R0

Made in the USA
Charleston, SC
03 April 2011